Don't get too close to the ginormous Gigantopithecus!

Watch out for the snapping jaws of Predator X!

Fly a Pteranodon around your room!

Explore the app to discover incredible facts and stats about the extinct animals!

THIS IS A CARLTON BOOK
Text, design and illustration © Carlton Books Limited 2017

Published in 2017 by Carlton Books Limited
An imprint of the Carlton Publishing Group
20 Mortimer Street, London W1T 3JW

A catalogue record for this book is
available from the British Library.

ISBN: 978-1-78312-254-7
Printed in Dongguan, China

Executive Editor: Jo Casey
Design Manager: Emily Clarke
Design and diagrams: WildPixel Ltd.
Cover illustration: WildPixel Ltd.
Digital Producer: Sean Daly
Picture research: Steve Behan
Production: Yael Steinitz

PICTURE CREDITS

Need some help? Check out our useful website
for helpful tips and problem-solving advice:
www.icarlton.co.uk/help

iEXPLORE

EXTINCT ANIMALS

Camilla de la Bédoyère

CARLTON
KIDS

GOING, GOING, GONE!

There has been animal life on Earth for about 600 million years. During that time, more than 90 per cent of all animal types, or species, that have ever lived have become extinct.

MASS EXTINCTION EVENTS

Occasionally, catastrophic events have occurred on Earth that have changed the world's climate and habitat and caused a massive number of extinctions. These are called mass extinction events. The disappearance of the dinosaurs around 65 million years ago is the most famous example.

ALL CHANGE

Extinction is mostly a normal and natural part of how life on Earth changes over time. A species dies out because it is no longer able to survive, but other species are able to. These animals thrive and continue to change and pass their survival skills on to their young until, one day, they also become extinct. This process is called natural selection and it's part of evolution – the way that living things change and adapt over generations and over time.

360 million years ago
Late Devonian Mass Extinction Much of the oxygen in the oceans disappeared and 70% of marine species became extinct.

500 million

440 million

400 million

360 million

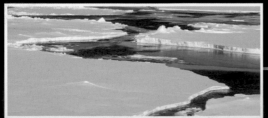

440 million years ago
The Big Freeze
The world's climate changed and turned cold. Large parts of land and sea were covered in ice and 85% of marine species disappeared.

MODERN EXTINCTIONS

Humans have proved, so far, to be one of the most successful animals to have evolved. We haven't just adapted to our environment – we've made it adapt to us. This has had a huge impact on the animals and plants we share the planet with. There are far more extinctions taking place and some scientists predict that, thanks to our pollution, habitat destruction, hunting and over-fishing, half of the world's marine and land species will be extinct 100 years from now. They suggest that humans are responsible for a current sixth mass extinction event.

UNCOVERING THE PAST

The mysterious past of extinct animals has been revealed by digging up their remains. Sometimes when animals died their bodies were covered by mud, sand or rock and, over millions of years, they were squashed and turned to stone. This is called fossilisation and the rocky remains are called fossils. Soft tissues, such as fur, skin or muscles, are rarely fossilised. More recently, animals such as dire wolves and woolly mammoths have been preserved in tar or ice. In these cases, soft tissues are often preserved.

200 million years ago
Triassic–Jurassic Mass Extinction
Floods of hot lava may have caused a colossal animal wipeout, but plants were not too badly affected.

250 million   200 million   100 million   65 million

250 million years ago
The Permian–Triassic Extinction
96% of species vanished, possibly following a comet impact, or a huge volcanic eruption. Life on Earth today is descended from the 4% of species that survived.

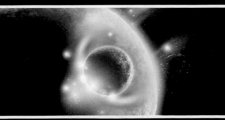

65 million years ago
The KT Event
A huge meteorite hit Mexico. The dinosaurs, as well as half of all species, died out.

PREDATOR X

Predator X was a deadly sea monster and one of the largest meat-eaters that ever lived. It patrolled the seas, using its powerful sense of smell to detect prey – just like today's sharks.

SUPER SPEED

Predator X was built for speed! With a bite force of about 15 tonnes (four times greater than that of the T-rex) it could easily crush large shelled ammonites and bones with a single snap. Once Predator X had its prey held tight in its teeth, it shook its head from side to side to kill it and loosen a chunk of flesh. This is similar to how modern sharks and crocodiles kill.

Predator X was a strong hunter with a deadly bite that could easily cut through muscle and bone.

WIPEOUT!

145 million years ago

EXTINCT ANIMALS
ACTIVATION PAGE

BRING IT BACK TO LIFE!
Watch out for the snapping jaws of Predator X!

Predator X fossils were discovered in 2006.

VITAL STATS

NAME:	Predator X or *Pliosaurus funkei*
SAY:	pligh-oh-saw-rus fun-kee
TYPE:	Marine reptile
WHERE:	European seas
WHEN:	Late Jurassic Epoch
SIZE:	

10–15 metres long

HUGE HEAD

Predator X had a large skull with long-toothed jaws that were 3 m in length. It had a streamlined body, two sets of flippers for swimming, and a strong, muscle-packed tail.

EARLY FOSSILS

Predator X was a pliosaur, a type of short-necked plesiosaur. Plesiosaurs were a group of huge swimming predators that were first unearthed about 200 years ago, before dinosaur fossils were discovered.

GUESSWORK

Scientists are still trying to find out how Predator X lived and when it died out. There is not much evidence to work from, but it may have lost out to mightier sea monsters called the mosasaurs, which were wiped out about 65 million years ago in the KT mass extinction event.

PTERANODON

When dinosaurs were masters of the Earth, massive flying reptiles ruled the skies. Known as pterosaurs, these animals were wiped out in the mass extinction that also saw the end of the dinosaurs 65 million years ago.

FLYING HIGH

The Pteranodon is probably the most famous of all the pterosaurs. It soared above the oceans, using its large eyes to look for fish to eat. It could flap its wings, but it saved energy by soaring on the wind to travel great distances at speed. It used its long, slender beak to scoop fish out of the water. On land, it walked on all four limbs.

TERRIFYING AND TOOTHLESS

Despite their bird-like appearance and flying skills, pterosaurs were not the ancestors of modern birds. Some had scales, while others had fur. Most pterosaurs had many teeth in their beak-like mouths, but Pteranodon was toothless.

Pteranodon walked using its wings.

CRAZY CREST

One of the great mysteries that surrounds Pteranodon is why it had a long, slender skull crest. Males had longer crests than females, so scientists think they may have played a part at mating time – just like the colourful feathers displayed by many modern male birds, such as peacocks.

A male's crest was as long as the rest of its skull.

GIGANTIC BUT GRACEFUL

Appearances can be deceptive, and the huge size of a Pteranodon makes it look heavy. In fact, like other pterosaurs, it had big bones but they were hollow. This made it much easier for the animal to get airborne.

EXTINCT ANIMALS
ACTIVATION PAGE

BRING IT BACK TO LIFE!
Make a terrifying Pteranodon soar around your room.

Its wings were made of a leathery, skin-like membrane.

VITAL STATS

NAME: *Pteranodon*

SAY: te-ran-oh-don

TYPE: Flying reptile

WHERE: North America and Europe

WHEN: Late Cretaceous Epoch

SIZE:

8 metres

WIPEOUT!

85

PARACERATHERIUM

At a colossal 20 tonnes, the mighty Paraceratherium weighed as much as four elephants and is the biggest land mammal yet discovered.

EXTINCT ANIMALS
ACTIVATION PAGE

BRING IT BACK TO LIFE!
See this massive
mammal up close!

RHINO OR HORSE?

This beast may look like a giant, muscular horse, but it was actually a hornless member of the rhinoceros family. Paraceratherium ate plants, like modern rhinos, and it could extend its long neck to reach a breathtaking height of 8 m to nibble leaves and twigs on trees.

ONCE COMMON

Around the time Paraceratherium lived there were many rhino species, and rhinos were still common in recent prehistory, living alongside our human ancestors. Today, there are just five rhino species and all of them are in danger of extinction. Modern rhinos are hunted for their horns, which some people mistakenly believe have magical or medicinal properties.

Paraceratherium's solid skull measured 140 cm long.

THICK-SKINNED

Like modern rhinos, Paraceratherium had thick skin and a powerful, stocky body. Its skull alone measured 140 cm long and was made of thick bone – which may have proved useful for headbutting during fights.

Despite being a rhino, Paraceratherium didn't have a horn, unlike modern rhinos.

VITAL STATS

NAME: *Paraceratherium*
SAY: para-sera-theer-ee-um
TYPE: Land mammal
WHERE: Europe to Asia

WHEN: Oligocene Epoch

SIZE:

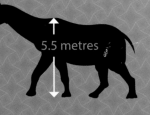

5.5 metres

WIPEOUT!

23
million
years ago

TOO BIG TO ATTACK

Paraceratherium probably lived a life similar to that of modern large herbivores, such as elephants. There would have been few predators willing to attack an adult. Youngsters, however, would have been more vulnerable so they might have needed to be protected by a herd.

MEGALODON

This prehistoric shark was colossal, quick and equipped with massive jaws. One bite from this mega marine predator was powerful enough to make mincemeat of a turtle or even a whale.

TOTALLY TOOTHSOME

There aren't many clues about Megalodon – only a few fossilised bones and lots of fossilised teeth. From these fossils scientists have calculated that it was about four times longer than a great white shark, and thirty times its weight. Megalodon probably hunted in a similar way to great white sharks by stalking its prey from below. It would swim towards its prey really fast and strike a body blow that would leave the victim defenceless against its huge serrated teeth.

Megalodon means 'big tooth'. It had deadly rows of sharp teeth that could grow up to 21 cm long and 10 cm wide at the base.

A REAL SOFTY

Like other sharks, Megalodon's skeleton was made of cartilage – a bone-like substance that is softer than bone, so it doesn't often fossilise well.

WIPEOUT!

2

SHARK FRIENDS

Although great white sharks are relatives of Megalodon and give scientists many clues about how these long-extinct animals may have lived, they are not descended from them. Great white sharks actually evolved around 11 million years ago, which means they were alive at the same time as Megalodon.

EXTINCT ANIMALS
ACTIVATION PAGE

BRING IT BACK TO LIFE!
Avoid Megalodon's mighty jaws!

RAN OUT OF FOOD?

No one knows why Megalodon became extinct, but it may have struggled to survive when the world's oceans cooled 2 million years ago, and there were fewer marine mammals to hunt. Great white sharks survived because they hunt different prey, and evolved the ability to keep their bodies warmer than the surrounding water.

GIGANTOPITHECUS

It's possible that our early human relatives came face to face with this huge prehistoric ape in ancient tropical forests. It would have been a terrifying sight!

DRAGGING ITS KNUCKLES

Scientists think that Gigantopithecus apes survived for about 8 million years. They have used fossilised bones to calculate that, although an adult might have stood 3 m tall, it probably walked on its feet and knuckles like gorillas, chimps and orang-utans.

WIPEOUT!

100,000
years ago

Fossilised teeth have provided clues about what the giant ape ate.

NOT ENOUGH ENERGY

Although large dinosaurs ruled the world for tens of millions of years, the largest land mammals survived for much shorter times. Mammals need energy to keep warm and to fuel their big brains, and if they have large bodies their energy needs are even greater. Generally, the larger a species becomes, the more likely it is to die out.

TOO BIG TO CLIMB

Gigantopithecus ate a diet of fruit and other plant material, but adults would have been too large to climb trees. As the world's climate changed, the ape's forest habitat became grassland, with fewer fruit trees. Gigantopithecus probably struggled to adapt to these new conditions and find enough food to survive, and so it eventually disappeared.

EXTINCT ANIMALS
ACTIVATION PAGE

BRING IT BACK TO LIFE!
Meet the ginormous
Gigantopithecus!

HUMAN INTERFERENCE

Orang-utans are facing extinction today. However, their forests are not disappearing because of a natural change in climate, but because humans cut them down. The stripped land is used to grow palm trees, which are a source of palm oil. Palm oil is used as vehicle or cooking fuel, in shampoo and in many foods.

SMILODON

With its ferocious fangs and powerful, muscular body, Smilodon might have been an incredible killing machine. However, its bite may not have been quite as impressive as it appears...

DAGGER TEETH

Smilodons are also known as sabre-toothed cats – named after their two dagger-like canine teeth, which could reach a terrifying 18 cm long! Smilodons were amongst the largest members of the cat family to ever live.

GROUP HUNTERS?

Big stocky cats often hunt by ambush. They hide in trees or under shrubs, before leaping out on their prey, and it's possible that this is how Smilodon caught its food. Some scientists argue that Smilodon hunted on grasslands instead. Like lions, a group could have worked together to chase and attack huge animals, such as mastodons, ground sloths and horses. Once caught, the prey animal would be killed by a swift bite to the throat. However, this mega-cat didn't have much power in its jaws – recent calculations suggest it had a bite force one third that of modern lions!

Smilodon's long canine teeth could easily stab prey, but they weren't strong enough to break through bone.

Smilodon used its heavy, muscular body to wrestle prey to the ground.

EXTINCT ANIMALS
ACTIVATION PAGE

BRING IT BACK TO LIFE!
Don't get too close to Smilodon's ferocious fangs!

NAME: *Smilodon*

SAY: smeye-loh-don

TYPE: Cat

WHERE: The Americas

WHEN: Pleistocene to early Holocene Epochs

SIZE:

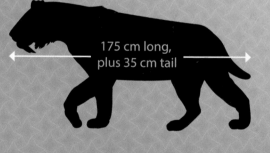

175 cm long, plus 35 cm tail

NOT GOOD ENOUGH

There were three species of Smilodon and they survived for about 2.5 million years. They became extinct as a result of climate change at the end of the last Ice Age, and were probably not as successful at hunting as other predators that survived.

FAST-GROWING FANGS

A young Smilodon's teeth grew at a rate of 6 mm a month. That's about twice as fast as modern cats' teeth grow. The teeth weren't fully grown until the youngster was about three years old, which means that cubs probably practised their hunting skills on small animals, and relied on adults to provide them with food.

DIRE WOLF

Imagine a pack of 20 massive snarling wolves with saliva dripping from their fangs as they paw the ground ready to leap. It's a terrifying image, and one that our human ancestors probably faced when they were on hunting expeditions!

TEAMWORK

The dire wolf's favourite prey included a group of animals called megaherbivores (giant plant-eaters), such as sloths, mammoths and bison. Catching and killing these powerful animals would only have been possible with the dire wolves working together in a pack, like grey wolves and other members of the dog family do today. This behaviour suggests that the dire wolf was a sociable, intelligent animal with good communication skills.

By analysing their bones, scientists have discovered that dire wolves mostly ate bison and horses.

TRAPPED IN TAR

The remains of more than 4,000 dire wolves have been found in La Brea Tar Pits in North America. Long ago, grazing animals became trapped in the gooey tar and predators, such as the dire wolf, coyotes and Smilodon, clambered on to the tar to reach them. These animals were also trapped, and died there. Scientists have collected more than 1 million bones, from 600 species of animal, from the pits.

ADAPTABLE

Like grey wolves, the dire wolf seems to have been very adaptable and able to live in a range of habitats, from forests to open grasslands. However, its survival skills were not good enough to cope with changes around 12,000 years ago, and it died out.

WIPEOUT!

12,000 years ago

VITAL STATS

NAME:	Dire wolf or *Canis dirus*
SAY:	ca-niss di-rus
TYPE:	Dog
WHERE:	The Americas
WHEN:	Pleistocene Epoch
SIZE:	

125 cm long, plus 63 cm tail

EXTINCT ANIMALS
ACTIVATION PAGE

BRING IT BACK TO LIFE!
Beware the
snarling dire wolf!

TOP DOGS

Curiously, although the dire wolf died out, grey wolves grew in number. No one knows why the dire wolf lost the battle for survival, but grey wolves were able to take over as top dogs.

MEGATHERIUM

Megatherium means 'giant beast' – and it was certainly massive! In fact, Megatherium was one of the biggest land mammals to ever live – similar in weight to an elephant.

WALKING GIANTS

Megatherium was one of a group of huge animals called ground sloths. They evolved in South America, during the time that this continent was an island. When a land bridge developed between South and North America, around 12 to 15 million years ago, ground sloths were able to move northwards.

Megatherium's claws could grow up to 50 cm long.

GOOD CHEWERS

Scientists know that Megatherium ate plants from studying its skull, jawbones and teeth. Plants are very hard to chew into a mash, so herbivores need large jaw and cheek muscles and broad molars for grinding. Meat-eaters have sharper teeth for piercing and slicing flesh. Some scientists think Megatherium may have occasionally attacked other animals, or scavenged food from dead creatures.

STANDING TALL

Like a bear, Megatherium could walk on four legs or two, and it could stand up tall to reach the juiciest leaves in a tree. It pulled down branches with its long, dagger-like claws, which it might also have used to climb.

VITAL STATS

NAME: *Megatherium*
SAY: mega-theer-ee-um
TYPE: Sloth
WHERE: The Americas

WHEN: Pliocene to early Holocene Epochs

SIZE:

6 metres

EXTINCT ANIMALS
ACTIVATION PAGE

BRING IT BACK TO LIFE!
Watch Megatherium walk around your room!

WIPEOUT!

10,500
years ago

LARGER THAN LIFE

Megatherium is one of a group of animals called the Pleistocene megafauna (giant animals). These were unusually large mammals that became extinct over a period of time known as the Quaternary extinction event. They may have become extinct as a result of climate change when the world warmed up, or because humans hunted them.

WOOLLY MAMMOTH

Woolly mammoths lived 58 million years ago and were the first elephant-like animals. This group of animals has survived until today, although many elephant species have become extinct along the way – including the woolly mammoth.

WIPEOUT!
5,700 years ago

WARM AND COSY

The woolly mammoth was well equipped to survive the cold and snow. It had a thick coat of fur with hair 1 m long, and its ears were smaller than modern elephants, so it was less likely to suffer from frostbite. Mammoths lived like elephants do today: roaming their habitat in family herds and grazing on plants.

FROZEN FLESH

When woolly mammoths died, their bodies were often quickly covered in sediment and ice, and remained frozen. Their flesh, bones and fur have survived to tell the story of their lives – and deaths.

EXTINCT ANIMALS
ACTIVATION PAGE

BRING IT BACK TO LIFE!
See this huge woolly mammoth in action!

HUNTED BY HUMANS

Humans and woolly mammoths lived alongside one another, and pictures of the big beasts have been found in caves where humans lived. It's likely that humans contributed to their extinction by hunting them. Most woolly mammoths had died out by 9,000 years ago, but some small groups were still alive on a remote island off the coast of Alaska less than 6,000 years ago.

Large curved tusks may have been used for fighting and for foraging for food.

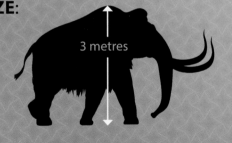
MODERN MAMMOTHS

There are three types of modern elephant: African savannah elephants and forest elephants, and smaller Asian elephants. Mammoths were most closely related to Asian elephants. All three elephant species are now in danger of extinction, having been hunted for the ivory in their tusks, which is highly valued by some people.

IRISH ELK

This magnificent beast was big, beautiful and fast. Irish elk lived in herds, like other deer, and could turn on the speed when attacked.

MATING MALES

Only male Irish elk possessed the distinctive antlers, which were made of bone. Every year male deer grew new antlers in time for the mating season, and lost them soon after.

SHOWING OFF

Deer use their antlers to fight each other, especially at mating time when males compete for females. Very large antlers, however, may not have been better weapons than smaller ones. In fact, they would have been so heavy that they might have made fighting difficult! Antlers may have a more useful job to do: large antlers demonstrate to other males that their owner is fit, healthy and strong, and too dangerous to fight. It also makes them more attractive to females. So, males with large antlers would be more likely to mate, and their young would inherit large antlers too.

WIDE LOAD

Irish elk antlers – which spanned a colossal 3 m or more across – may have contributed to their extinction. The landscape at the time was becoming more forested, and a large deer with huge headgear may have found it difficult to move easily through trees and shrubs. The Irish elk's close relatives, such as fallow deer, reindeer and red deer, thrived and are still common in many parts of Europe today.

The Irish elk is one of the largest deer that ever lived.

EXTINCT ANIMALS
ACTIVATION PAGE

BRING IT BACK TO LIFE!
Watch out for the Irish elk's antlers!

VITAL STATS

NAME: Irish elk or *Megaloceros*
SAY: meg-a-loh-ser-os
TYPE: Deer
WHERE: Europe and northern Asia

WHEN: Pleistocene and early Holocene Epochs

SIZE:

2 metres

HUMAN IMPACT

The Irish elk died out when the climate changed, and the impact of humans in its habitat drove many species to extinction.

TASMANIAN TIGER

This cat-like beast was more closely related to the Tasmanian devil than to tigers or lions. It was Australia's largest predator until around 3,500 years ago.

TIMID TIGER

A shy, secretive creature, the Tasmanian tiger became extinct before scientists had an opportunity to study its lifestyle. It was a marsupial that lived in forests and was nocturnal, which means that it was most active at night, and slept in the daytime.

POUCH BABIES

Marsupials are mammals that give birth to very small young, which then develop and grow inside a pouch on their mother's body, suckling on her milk. Kangaroos, koalas and wombats are marsupials of Australia. Opossums are marsupials of the Americas.

HUMAN ACTIVITY

Tasmanian tigers died out in mainland Australia and New Guinea about 2,000 years ago, when humans invaded their habitats. They survived until the 1930s on the island of Tasmania. They finally became extinct after being hunted – often by farmers who blamed the tigers for killing their sheep. Farmers also introduced dogs to the island and they may have killed the marsupials and spread new diseases.

EXTINCT ANIMALS
ACTIVATION PAGE

BRING IT BACK TO LIFE!
See a snarling
Tasmanian tiger!

NAME: Tasmanian tiger or *Thylacine*

SAY: thigh-la-seen

TYPE: Marsupial

WHERE: Australia, Tasmania and New Guinea

WHEN: Holocene Epoch

SIZE:

130 cm long, plus 50 cm tail

NOT EXTINCT?

The Tasmanian tiger was declared extinct in 1986; however some people believe that it still exists and there have been many reports of sightings since the 1930s, although none has been proved. It's often difficult to state exactly when a species has gone extinct – but in our modern world it is easy to identify thousands of species that are now in danger of extinction because of human activity.

FUN FACTS!

Fossilised poo can be used to work out what extinct animals may have eaten.

In the future it may be possible to use mammoths' frozen body tissues to recreate these extinct mammals so they can live again.

Despite its huge size, Gigantopithecus might have only showed its brute strength when it, or its family, was in danger – just like modern gorillas.

The word 'sloth' is used for a person or animal that does not move quickly, and fossil evidence suggests that giant sloths could walk, but not run.

Smilodons could open their mouths twice as wide as modern lions.

The first person to discover the fossilised remains of a plesiosaur was a young English woman called Mary Anning in 1821.

Today, more than one third of all mammal species are threatened with extinction. More than half of all frog and toad species are in deadly danger of dying out forever.